IN THE QUAKER HOTEL

Helen Tookey was born near Leicester in 1969. She is now based in Liverpool, where she teaches creative writing at Liverpool John Moores University. She studied philosophy and English literature at university, and has published critical work about writers including Anaïs Nin and Malcolm Lowry. Her debut collection *Missel-Child* (Carcanet, 2014) was shortlisted for the Seamus Heaney First Collection Prize; her second collection *City of Departures* (Carcanet, 2019) was shortlisted for the Forward Prize for Best Collection.

In the Quaker Hotel

Helen Tookey

CARCANET POETRY

First published in Great Britain in 2022 by
Carcanet
Alliance House, 30 Cross Street
Manchester, M2 7AQ
www.carcanet.co.uk

A CIP catalogue record for this book is
available from the British Library.

ISBN 978 1 80017 182 4

Book design by Andrew Latimer
Printed in Great Britain by SRP Ltd, Exeter, Devon

The publisher acknowledges financial
assistance from Arts Council England.

Contents

NOVA SCOTIA

UNCHARTED

IN THE QUAKER HOTEL

A PICTURE WINDOW

UNDER THE LIGHTSHIP

The lightship rides at the top of the cliff,
just beyond the promenade.
No one remembers when it came
nor can they read the white name
painted backwards on its hull.

The town lives below the ship
submerged in the blue of early dusk
or the hour before sun-up,
rattle of laughter and breaking glass
rising in the narrow air
between the tall white guest-houses,
no vacancies, monochrome fuzz
of small TVs on kitchen tables.

Someone has cut a hole in the town,
a picture window onto a beach
very early, pale gold streaks
on the water, and black rocks,
or maybe islands (the scale is tricky)
somewhere surely far to the north.
The people are sleeping, a long time ago,
but dawn is coming up like fire
under the lightship, pouring through
the cracks in the town, too fast,
too soon, too bright to be borne.

AMBER

When they told us the insects were dying
we finally understood it was over. We didn't know how
to tell the children, went out for a walk
by the long edge of the playing-fields. The sky
was yellow. Sundays had always tasted of sorrow
but this was different. We remembered
the beach by the glass-green water,
how Sarah had found the huge chunk of amber,
lugged it up to the hut on the prom to show Theo
the lifeguard, the rest of us crowding, trying to prove
we were part of the finding, and every day for the rest of the summer
we scoured the tideline for yellow pebbles, desperately wanting
them to be amber, and when summer was over
we put the beach in our pockets and went back to school.

RIVER OAKS

The fountain in the memorial garden
is still in perfect working order
but the playground is gone. Derelict already

last time you were here, it's now fenced off,
slide and swings and ride-on animals
ripped out, disappeared. A small earth-mover

and sacks of cement wait hopefully.
Did the children all grow up and move away?
The elegant houses are saying nothing.

In the memorial garden, pansies and zinnias
are flourishing. Each rosebush
carries its nameplate: *Waltz Time. Compassion.*

Eyes for You. The bench on the decking
overlooking the pond has a brass plaque
let into its framework: *River Oaks*

Residents' Association. You peer down
at the shallow water, looking for fish,
but don't see any. Sunlight dazzles,

flashes off the surface like a signal off a mirror,
a message sent across some vast distance.
Much too late by the time you receive it.

IN THE QUAKER HOTEL

single room on the top floor
narrow bed   plain white bedspread

ventilator hum like a ship's distant engines
floorboard creak

the brochure suggests *a retreat for enquirers*
could I learn to *experiment with light?*

can be challenging   the writer warns
but may lead to new growth

below the window   communal gardens
flagged square with two beehives

a kind of altar   it comes to me
bees the tiny gods we depend on

each of us at our glowing window
a very practical discipline

WALKING IN THE WOODS WITH SARAH

not a path

softness underfoot
orange-brown compression layer
needles   pinecones   breaking down
becoming what

no roots no shadows

daub of bright neon green
at the base of each trunk

she said unmoored   unlocated
not sure which way is up

she said cold hands   knucklegrowths
soft tissue decay   a thinning-out

I said certain unwantings   undefinings
a kind of walking out of oneself

wandering the woods' soft body

exposed roots   ribs of a boat
ribs of a former animal

at the edge of the trees   sandy earth

asparagus fields
running for miles behind the dunes

not a loss
something like a clarifying
becoming something you can't name

ASHES IN THE WATER

Ashes in the water, ashes in the sea
We all jump up with a one, two, three

Walking to the station, overhearing children in a garden chanting the rhyme. But they didn't know it was *ashes*, so they said *fishes. Fishes in the water, fishes in the sea.* Of course that would make sense, what would you expect to find in the sea but fishes?

*

Those photographs last winter, the skies deep orange, the people huddled in their hundreds on the beaches, cloth tied round their faces. Nowhere to go but the beach and then, the ones who could, taking to the sea in small boats, days and nights just sitting there on the water in the orange half-dark, waiting, not knowing if the fires would ever be put out, if the skies and the air would ever clear.

*

Walking on the narrow strip of beach at Caldy – three, four, years ago? The continuous crunch of our footsteps over fragments of shell, millions of them. Suddenly seeing this strip of shore as a boneyard, a reliquary.

*

As a child, hunkered by the tidepools, gazing down at their miniature worlds. The small darting transparent creatures, how strange that creatures could look like that, as though made only of the water they swam in. The waving fronds of the anemones, dark-red, blood-red, daring to put your finger against them and feel all the tentacles instantly grip, latch with toy-like force against your skin. And on the floor of the pool, beneath the clear water, the jewel-like fragments of stone, and the strange smooth white flakes that you thought of as bone, thin white chips like porcelain, their edges smoothed off by the water. You collected them as though they were some kind of currency, not realising that they were fragments of shell, that they too had once held living creatures.

*

You finally as a handful of grit, a handful of ash, scattered in the tidepools, sinking down through the shallow water, coming to rest among the fragments of stone, fragments of shell and bone and porcelain, you finally part of this world you have looked at for so long, but could you know it?

NEW BRIGHTON / AUGUST

This place again – odd angle
where land meets water, river

turns sea. Tide going out fast,
riffling backwards

over ridged brown sand.
Straight ahead, wind turbines

pecking at the water
like tall white wading birds.

Guarding the river, the shut fort,
built for an invasion

that never happened. Sandstone hull
sunk in the sand, superstructure

twisted, tilting – radar antennae
still turning, still listening

though to what signals, and who
could be there to receive, decipher –

Fifty yards further out,
the lighthouse, still elegant,

white paint only a little
rust-stained, low down

where the iron ladder clings
to the side, climbs up

to the recessed doorway's
dark slot. Thirty lamps,

three fog bells, stripped out
years ago – now pigeons nest

in the roof-beams, dive and flutter
the lantern-room, as though trying

to catch our attention – look
at what's no longer here, are you sure

you won't be glad of them, those lamps
and bells, when your satellites

have all blinked out, when your radio's
full of empty air –

HOSPITALITY OF WATER

LONG GRASS WITH BUTTERFLIES

They encourage me to walk in the gardens
but they won't allow me to stop and look.
They crowd me, they hold up constantly
their small devices. The grass grows
tall and unkempt – granted, it seems,
a certain freedom. Their devices tell them
how to see. They don't allow me
to see with my eyes – the nakedness,
they find it obscene. In the long grass
are butterflies, huge and violent. The trees
are cut off, close to the ground. The white path
leads into the trees, and disappears.

SEASONS OF THE HOSPITAL

A long building, yellowish. Shutters
of bright acid green. Low to the left
a woman walks in a long grey dress,
her red umbrella blown inside-out.
Pines and cedars curling upwards
over her head, twining together
in hectic space.

*

These blue bodies, misshapen gods
alone in the cornfield. Sagging
under the weight of themselves, hung
from the wires of their own green shoots.
Sunset, everything burning, and these three
left in the cornfield to save themselves
as best they can.

*

Turned earth, pale with frost –
pinks, blues, candy colours. Trunk of the yew
in extreme close-up, its patternings
also pale with cold. Long cut of canal
and towpath. Low roofs of the town beyond,
and over it all the heavy yellow
word of the sky.

*

No colour here, in this scrubby
overlooked corner of the garden – a scene
already half-erased. A choked pond,
a wooden fence, and this solitary man
hunched over a spade, petitioning
the cast-off ground. Hoping maybe
something might grow.

CORRIDOR

We stand as though we're about to dive. The corridor is infinite, stretches away from us forever. How did you know it so exactly, I say. I had thought it was my dream only. I've lived here for years, he says. Ribbed with archways overhead, purplish, pale pink. Small shimmering patches of blue, toothache-bright. Migraine light. Canyoned, cracked across, the floor yaws. To our right the beginnings of a stairway, huge high marble cliffs we know we could never possibly climb. Far in the distance, a small man is hurrying, about to open a door and vanish, though he doesn't vanish, he stays where he is, fixed in his hurry. The small man's where we will be soon, only we can't move. Eventually, though, we will move, because we can't go back, *back* has closed behind us like the silver of a mirror. We stand as though we're about to dive. He takes my hand. *Now*, he says, and we step forward.

CYPRESS

It's a black flame, a fire-tree
that gives no light, that burns
in a cold agony all night on the hill.

Tall thin winding tower
piercing the sky, mocking the calm
blue-grey spire of the church below

– some kind of a horrible miracle,
this black flame that won't burn out,
that writhes in the cold space of itself

like the constant anxious washing of hands.
Why did you show me, why did you bring me
here to this place? Now the cypress burns

in my mind too, and the stars spin
like catherine wheels, vast and white
and pitiless, and none of it seen,

none of it dreamed down in the valley,
by the small blue town, sleeping.

dream of breaking the skin of water
drop down through its green body

hospitality of water:
displacement / recalibration

two-way negotiation
continual exchange across soft borders

TRACK

[first day]

We walked out in the morning, the four of us. By agreement we walked without speaking, followed the track past the wheatfields down to the canal. Sun behind a shirr of cloud. Everything warm and moving. Brown sparrows dancing in pairs over the wheat, seeming to sit and ride on the surface of it, flushing up in mild alarm as we passed. The wheat an almost-solid surface, long spikes on each ear forming a kind of frothy blanket that rustled in the wind, the small birds playing and resting on this. We by contrast too large, out of scale with the world around us. How might we shrink ourselves down?

[second day]

Sun still low but already fierce, thin cloud burned away early, and the warm wind already strong. We walked with the wheatfield to our left; to our right, long rows of sunflower plants. The oil we need to cook our food, to keep our machines running. On this day we saw no animals. But I had heard them in the night, skittering overhead, and they found their way into my dream – animals kept from earlier times, in long rows of cages, ready to be let out again when conditions were suitable. Only somehow they had got out already, everything was in complete confusion, no one knowing what to do.

[third day]

This day on the track things seemed different. Scent of water, clods of earth where some vehicle had passed earlier – leaving its trail, like a kind of animal. Four of us as before, but this time I was walking ahead. Disconcerting, knowing the others were following me but not being able to see them. I could hear their presence in small sounds – their footsteps on the road, the clinking of a metal water bottle. As we got nearer to the bridge I began to feel the not-seeing as a kind of pressure, I began to want to turn round and look. But I felt I was under an interdiction, that looking round was not permitted, would result in some kind of catastrophe.

[fourth day]

I walked alone down the track to the canal. The question being asked was that of heat. The wind had risen again overnight, hot and dry. The wheat hissing, as though in disapproval, and from overhead a strange humming sound, a kind of low-pitched wordless singing – the sound of the wind in the telegraph wires. By the canal, below the lock, I sat in the long grass, in the shade of the trees. A butterfly landed on my arm and stayed there for quite a while, walking in circles, its wings folded: pale brown and yellowish, with a single small black spot on each wing. I could just feel its movements against my skin.

On the way back along the track, a black glint – I thought at first a piece of black glass, but was puzzled by its roundness, a tiny black glass ball. Looking more closely I saw there were others, bubbles forming in the patches of tar on the road surface, perfect spheres of near-liquid black, and at the centre of each, a reddish-gold gleam, like garnet – the surface of the track beginning to melt, turning back to liquid oil.

POOL / OTHER BODY

trying to rescue the drowning wasps
trapped & held by surface tension

for them solid   for us a membrane
offering only slight resistance

strange band of flickering white
around my wrist as it crossed the threshold

looking down at my other body
shadow   reflection   uncertain exactly

what I was seeing   but recognising
a kind of encounter

what if that space could be opened up
boundary become a holding zone

in which two selves met & somehow didn't
dissolve in each other

wasps drowning the rescue to trying
tension surface by held & trapped

membrane a us for   solid them for
resistance slight only offering

white flickering of band strange
threshold the crossed it as wrist my around

body other my at down looking
exactly uncertain   reflection   shadow

recognising but   seeing was I what
encounter of kind a

up opened be could space that if what
zone holding a become boundary

didn't somehow & met selves two which in
other each in dissolve

dissolve in each other
in which two selves met & somehow didn't

boundary become a holding zone
what if that space could be opened up

a kind of encounter
what I was seeing   but recognising

shadow   reflection   uncertain exactly
looking down at my other body

around my wrist as it crossed the threshold
strange band of flickering white

offering only slight resistance
for them solid   for us a membrane

trapped & held by surface tension
trying to rescue the drowning wasps

other each in dissolve
didn't somehow & met selves two which in

zone holding a become boundary
up opened be could space that if what

encounter of kind a
recognising but   seeing was I what

exactly uncertain   reflection   shadow
body other my at down looking

threshold the crossed it as wrist my around
white flickering of band strange

resistance slight only offering
membrane a us for   solid them for

tension surface by held & trapped
wasps drowning the rescue to trying

RUE DE LA GRAVIÈRE

Last year's leaves, brittle as parchment,
rattle in the breeze, break up underfoot.
The lavender too is dry and brittle,

long mauve spikes of the flowerheads
rough to the touch, crumbling a little
between finger and thumb

but the scent still released to your skin,
clean, sharp, medicinal. Bells ring
from the church in the village

though the abbey is silent, keeps its secrets
– *Domaine Privé* warns the sign –
so you take the track out through the fields,

Rue de la Gravière, street of the gravel-pit,
shallow fold in the field-line
showing where they dug the stone.

(Pick up a piece of white quartz,
remember your dream of the mason's yard,
crushed marble glittering,

the stone-cutter white with dust,
agitation of hands, some message
you couldn't grasp.) Cross the road

at the end of the track, push open
the heavy gate to the cemetery.
Family plots with ceramic roses,

wildflowers pressed into yellow plastic.
Dans notre cœur, tu demeures.
In the north-east corner the plain graves,

flotilla of small stone sails
for those without family, those without names
and here now this green lizard

darting across the speckled granite
in a flicker of limbs, like the people in the old films
stepping forever as though towards you,

hurrying past, and out of the frame.

lightbox
the pool at night
unfamiliar gleaming things

oblong of glowing colour
made us other
inside the water

CONCESSION À PERPETUITÉ

the words incised on the family tombs

CONCESSION A PERPETUITÉ
CONCESSION PERPÉTUELLE

*

concession:

– *a thing that is granted, especially in response to demands*
– *the action of conceding or granting something*
– *a gesture made in recognition of a demand or prevailing standard*
– *a preferential allowance or rate given by an organization*
– *the right to use land or other property for a specified purpose, granted by a government, company, or other controlling body*
– *a piece of land into which surveyed land is divided*

from Latin concedere, from con 'completely' + cedere 'to yield'

*

Qu'est-ce qu'une concession funéraire?
Une concession funéraire est un emplacement dans un cimetière (caveau, tombe)

a plot in a cemetery (vault, tomb)

dont vous achetez l'usage

of which you purchase the use

(mais non le terrain)

(but not the terrain)

terrain / ground / territory
earth

*

— a thing that is granted, especially in response to demands
— the action of conceding or granting something

a question then of who holds the power
and under what conditions
and for how long

*

Plusieurs durées de concession peuvent être accordées

several durations / lengths of concession may be accorded

accorded / awarded / bestowed / granted
(a gesture made in recognition)

− Concession temporaire : entre 5 ans et 15 ans
− Concession trentenaire : 30 ans
− Concession cinquantenaire : 50 ans
− Concession perpétuelle : durée illimitée

unlimited duration

world without end?

*

La commune peut-elle reprendre une concession?

*Can the town [authorities] rescind / repeal / take back a
concession?*

Oui, dans 2 cas.
– Non-renonvellement d'une concession à durée limitée
– Concession en état d'abandon

in a state / condition of [being] abandon[ed]

responsibility not having been taken
things having been allowed to fall into disrepair
having become overgrown / choked / damaged / broken

resulting in a state of decay / decadence / abandonment

the authorities then liable to intervene
rescind / retract / withdraw the concession

*

so easy to forget   to let things slide
to let the conditions slip your mind

go back   read the small print

*dont vous achetez l'usage
(mais non le terrain)*

SUDLEY FIELD

this small field   it has become
a clockwise habit   a repeated enquiry

what am I asking?

*

Slip through the gap in the sandstone wall and the field opens
up. The space of sky that suddenly appears. The air different,
cooler and fresher, the heat not trapped by the hard surfaces
of the streets. Walk up the earth path, under the beech trees,
along by the sandstone wall. The sight and scent of green,
dense shifting space of nettles and ivy. And then out from the
trees by the stone steps, the merchant's house, and the gate to
the rose garden, standing open –

*

the path through the trees a cloister of birds

seek the green chapel

weave & cross-cut of song overhead
for the time it takes to walk the path

*

Fallen tree like a sad beast, twisted roots of ivy behind the garden wall. Envelope of ashes and charred Swan Vestas, protective cross of rowan wood. The way the green gate opens to the rose garden, standing invitation to a place of memory. The six white rose-trees and the surrounding red, and the sad scarf on the sundial.

*

Walking for once anticlockwise, turning right, not left, towards the infant trees – oak, beech, rowan, planted maybe five years ago, at first just foot-high shoots, now already taller than me, and already too crowded, clamouring for attention in their small patch of ground. Surprised by how disorienting it feels – the field on my wrong side, not speaking to me.

*

The garden as stage set. The gates standing open, the benches on the veranda inviting you. Unsure whether you are audience or actor, taking your seat, waiting. After a while, sensing it, like a rustle of silk, a restlessness. Presence of a question: what might you make of this place? or what might it make of you?

*

Earth path now covered with fallen leaves. Air still and grey, cloud low over the estuary. Sense of being held, of waiting for something. The weather not yet harsh, but we know it will come.

*

only the field
& the high song of the wind in the beech trees
& the gulls   scraps of being   blown down the wind
crazy chase of sky over river
gleam of sunlight on gunmetal water
there and gone as clouds shift
gulls white against field   black against sky
& the wind in the beech trees   immense as ocean
so you cry aloud into the sound of it
and the rain comes the rain comes the rain comes

*

The veranda roof is leaking. One of the skylight panes is cracked. And the putty round the edges of the panes is old, dried up, shrinking away from the edges, no longer making a good seal between glass and wood, blackened with mould. The glass panes themselves are speckled and greened with moss. Rain drips onto the mosaic floor, onto the wooden benches. Somewhere between inside and outside, shelter and not.

*

what is it   this desire for a simple thing
a stone   a tree   birdsong
a field of course is not simple but you want it to be

come at it a different way –
is this where you lose language   empty your hands
a renunciation?

*

The small hearths built into the garden wall, to protect the
wintering plants against frost. The door behind the ivy, and
this small child, climbing the steps, calling back to the adults:
Come on! I'll show you the way!

*

Christmas day   & like an answer it is there
hawk in the beech tree
wings outstretched   black tips
you don't have the name   but you recognise its presence
takes to the air   branches spin against sky
as you try to track it
thirty seconds   but it was there
enough   that it was there

*

Thaw. Under the trees, earth-surface softened, uneasy underfoot. A kind of truce – uncertain which way to go. Thin water hanging in air. Damp patches on the benches from the leaking veranda roof. Something in the world keeps turning its face away.

*

February sun through thick cloud, cold flecks of rain in the air. New red leaves coming on the roses, still tight-furled against the wind but there, sharp new red, thin growth-lines from the blunt-cut tips of the grey-green stems. The man coming out to the courtyard to refill the bird feeder, telling me how to recognise a robin's song, telling me about the family of goldfinches he watches from his office window just above us.

*

Today everything moving, sailing. Gusty spring wind; under the beech trees quick play of light and shadow. On the earth path, a pair of blackbirds. The male almost at once flew up onto the ivy-covered wall, but the female stayed, pecking in the soft earth for grubs or worms. I waited, took my cue to move from her. She must have been aware of me, but seemed unfussed so long as I kept my distance. So I followed her slowly up the sloping path, until for whatever reason of her own she too flew up to the safety of the wall and the overhanging trees; and I saw that there was the male, having kept pace with her all the while, flitting unseen from tree to tree.

*

The beech tree doesn't recognise me as a person, or as anything at all. What then does it give me? Feeling of entering into communion, into relation, with some kind of entity, but there is nothing personal here. So the constraints of identity are loosened, for a while. A kind of going-out, almost being allowed into the impersonal being of the tree. I might say that the sound of the wind in the beech tree reminds me of the sea – but that is nothing to the beech tree.

*

Here on the veranda is where everything centres into itself. This is the only goal, the only explanation I could give you.

*

The cherry tree grows straight, then splits and twists, spirals into three, each bough with its abrupt angles, doublings-back, bark cracked at the knuckle-points – the tree's decisions and shifts of direction written on its skin, formed into its bone growth. I hold my notebook open beneath it, try to catch its drift.

*

on the earth path   this sense of placement
as though you were setting each foot naked on the earth
as though you came into a new kind of connection
your body moving inside air
things falling correctly

the space under the trees a kind of rightness

*

The pink cherry is full with blossom but the white is over.
Remembering how I stood inside its white vault, observed its
unfurling, layer on layer, yet there was always another closed
bud, always something further withheld. Today a kind of relief
in finding its beauty spoiled, its promise already past, not
holding.

*

under the trees   deep gloss of ivy
light-mottled leaves against the sky
underfoot beechmast   little   loose
dry   fourpointed   pale brown on the dry earth

emerge into the space of light
unrolling green   it opens to you
glasslike   jewel-like   yet a softness
a gathering   an altar cloth   scattered with leaves

like the floor of the chapel   where the swifts were
sudden   unexpected in their livingness
their dart & flicker   & coming to rest
making of the chapel   a new thing

*

Past nine pm. The whole field in shadow, and the sun blazing to
its setting an inch above the housetops. Sky in the west slants
of purple and gold. The low hills beyond the river distinct, blue-
grey, almost mauve, pink-orange gleams here and there as the
low sun catches buildings. The gunmetal stripe of the river. The
lovely music of the blackbirds, the low calls of the doves, and
the sky in the west goldening and pinking, bright gleaming
gold low down and above it a soft sheen of pinkish-blue-grey
like eyeshadow palettes, and the colours just changing slightly
as you look, as the gold sharpens and the black silhouettes of
trees and rooftops thicken and deepen, and the gold lights the
clouds from underneath, the mauve deepens like a sea, island
clouds of lighter pink, darker pink, and the Welsh hills now a
soft pink, clearly glowing above the dark blue of Wirral, and
the river's blue lighter by contrast. The undersides of all the
clouds now bright salmon pink, and the hills blueing from
below, just their very tops still pinkish, and the gold in the
west now fading and the air pressing colder around you –

*

Choreography of swallows – the risk & calculation, turning on a sixpence, wingtip/wingtip. Quick speech of the whole body, dark/bright, skimming the grass – six, seven, eight in conversation, configuring space above the ground of the field.

*

Sunday morning. Church bells in the distance. In the cathedral of beech trees, leaves falling, beginning to fall – the little skittering sounds of them –

And on the path just now, quick bright scraps of birds, flickering pale, red caps – the goldfinches –

STILLED IN A HALLWAY

LEAPFROG

Well, if you're going, I'm going

the small girl with dark hair exclaims
to her friend, on the lawn outside the café.
I mean, you can't play leapfrog on your own.

She's the one who's been making the rules,
orchestrating and shaping the game; the other girl's
just playing along. Her friend shrugs,

runs inside. She wants to know
what the adults are doing, she wants to sit
at the table with them, practise becoming

part of their world. Left alone, the smaller girl
kicks a little at the grass, then follows slowly.
I really like the game leapfrog, she states

decisively, to no one. Minutes later
she bursts back out through the French windows,
begins turning cartwheels the length of the lawn.

DOMINO: DES OISEAUX ET DES PAPILLONS

Small pieces of coloured card,
printed with birds and butterflies.
She plays by herself, trying to act

with scrupulous fairness
to each imaginary player in turn.
The creatures are beautifully drawn in ink,

their names printed underneath.
She enjoys saying the words,
the unfamiliar sounds in her mouth.

Bouvreuil is a round little bird
with a red breast and blue wings.
Cacatoès with his white crest

sticking up in crazy curls.
And *hirondelle* – she knows this one,
his long pointed wings and tail

making a shape that's nearly a star.
The butterflies seem trickier –
catogramme like a small black cloak,

callimorphe with its patternings
like camouflage, yellow and green,
red and black, as though it's half one thing

and half another. She goes on
placing the cards, making little murmurings
as the pattern turns, or comes to a halt.

Callimorphe. Cacatoès. Cacatoès. Bouvreuil.
She can't go. She stares down
at the fat little bird, his red breast,

his yellow tail. She fetches a pen,
neatly blinds him. Goodnight *bouvreuil.*
Then scribbles him out in black completely.

Summer stilled in a guest-house hallway. Sunlight shining on tiled floor. Red geraniums. Fat green glass globe – frog belly, bottle garden. Miniature forest. Tree creeper, white rocks, waterfalls. Sunlight shining. Split-second switch of attention. Tiled floor, seen from above. Black and white diamonds. Strange white eel shape, bent and twisted back on itself. Someone's arm, rippling as though underwater. Thin high stream of sound, sound pouring from someone's mouth.

*

Wake in a room with green walls, white ceiling. Flat on your back in a strange bed. Hard mattress, stiff sheets, pulled tight across your body, so tight you can't move. So white. Arm encased, hard and heavy, lying cold across your body. *Don't look, don't look down.* Eyes fixed on white ceiling.

Later, people. Words heard overhead: *greenstick fracture.* Imagining the bone in your arm as a soft stick, bent and fraying, not snapping clean underfoot. A green stick, good for nothing, rotting down on the forest floor.

*

Fat green glass globe. Bottle garden. Frog belly, holding a world. Summer seen through a green glass, stilled in a hallway. You on your haunches, face pressed to thick glass. Seeing yourself on the forest floor, tumbled among the white rocks, broken shells. Moss-slick. Heat-thick. Scrambling around inside the grottos, climbing the stone staircases. Stone throats, stone mouths dripping green. Waterfalls. Rock garden. Rainforest. Thick heat. Tree creeper crawling the walls. Small fists, banging the glass.

*

End of summer. They crack off the casing. Thin high whirring sound, tiny wings beating fast, too fast to see. Thin white stiff thing, lying dead in its broken cocoon. In the gardens, tired grass, dusty paths. Constant low background sound of falling water. *Try*, says the woman, *try to straighten it, just a little.* Shake your head. Stare at the fountain. Stare at the bronze animals. Eyes fixed on the pale water sparkling into bronze basins, gushing out from bronze mouths. Waterfalls. Bottle garden. Frog belly. Red geraniums. Summer stilled in a guest-house hallway. Sunlight shining on tiled floor.

POOL / CUT

the bright moons in the pool walls
the metal cages over their faces

the portholes of white light
pulling her inside their shine

the kick   the swift sting in her foot
the trail of blood on the white tiled floor

the small dark cinema room
the people falling through blue and green

the woman singing   her voice somehow
both angry and glad   *Nobody*

does it better   the fierce softness
like bleeding through water

The modern landscape, on the wall
next to the screen. The reassuring text.

It lasts 6 ½ minutes.
It restarts automatically.

Loss pulls. *The aurochs. The lynx. The brown bear.*
Allow the creature due respect.

Calm and slightly mesmerising, the voice of the woman
several times over.

Forests appear and disappear. Such a short space of time,
from the last Ice Age

to the present day. A six-minute film,
down in the basement.

BIRTHSTONE

It arrives in a plain envelope
a few days past the event.
Small dark red bead
on a thin chain.
Garnet. Your birthstone.

Remember how you stood
in the giftshops,
slowly turning the carousels.
You didn't want that bleak month,
that winter birth. You wanted
the summer gleam of amber.

Hold it up to the light
and a picture slides into your mind:
deep snow, trees like stone,
the sad young queen at her window.
Three bright stains already
on the white damask cloth she's sewing
and the slowly rounding red bead
at her pricked finger.

EMAIL FROM THE QUAKER HOTEL

All through the shut months
it keeps coming back to mind.
The quiet of the place. The plainness
of it.

Something there still to be found
but the email isn't a surprise

Unsustainable
Must relinquish the lease

A door closed on a small room,
a lighted window.
Wondering who will tend the bees
in the communal garden.

NEW BRIGHTON / NOVEMBER

The sea is nearly silent here,
sidling over the flat sand,
swelling itself against the seawall,

its surface close in oily-still,
greenish-dark, but further out
electric blue, shifting like static,

like detuned TV. There ought to be
another word for this sea you can't use,
deceptive place of sinking sand

and undertows. Maybe there is
and the lighthouse knows it, but won't tell,
standing there casting its white reflection

back to shore like an invitation,
as though to say *Come on, it's easy* –
and the long low container ships

sliding out on the tide, piled high
with their logical boxes, they know it too –
This place, they say smoothly, *is ours. Ours.*

NOVA SCOTIA

8740 HIGHWAY 2 GREAT VILLAGE

the house was a puzzle   it seemed so simple
small wooden box with a shiny roof

but nothing stayed in the same place
nothing was ever the same twice

everywhere windows and mirrors
reflections of windows in picture-glass

even the roof a kind of mirror
its tin shingles reflecting the weather

– bright as a knife in the afternoon sun
but in the half-light of dawn, like dirty snow

lying thin on winter earth

identical windows on all four sides
each looking out on a different road

– the road to Truro, to Londonderry
the road past the church, the bay road –

but directions seeming to switch about
as though the house had turned in the night

and pointed now to a different matter
– barometer, fortune-teller

like the tiny wooden weatherhouse
my grandmother kept on the windowsill

with its tiny people taking turns
to come out to consider the temperature

sit on their porch and predict the future

ECONOMY POINT

we took the path through the trees
to the wide red bay   soft mud
sucked at our boots   & the saltmarsh muttered
air bubbles pocking up   between thin green stems

the shoreline was strewn with the bones of trees
dragged out from the soft earth   bleached & dried
& flung back up in tangled heaps   common graves

at the headland the tide-carved ledges of rock
were easier walking   you went on ahead
fast   determined   & all the while turning your head
as though listening for something

the sandstone was scoured by swallowholes   small wells
of red water   I stopped to clean the weight
from my boots   clay slip
under my nails
                    – myself as a child
moulding earth into little bowls   setting them
to dry in the sun   though they never dried
enough to hold water –

the sound of the tide louder now   brightness sliding
over the mud   where we had walked

you lost to sight   & only the bay
looking back at me   – small creature
caught & held in its wide-angle stare

speck in the eye of this ancient place
of clay & water   scrabbling back
over glittering rock   to higher ground

ACADIA MINES

up in the mountains   the thin air
the gravel road   into the trees

we crossed the bridge over the falls
followed the track of the power lines

broken rock under our feet
mica   schist   glittering quartz

the air jittered   glitchy with static
yellow insects crackled & sparked

short-circuits in dry air
empty air   everything off-station

we were looking for the fault   the tripping switch
the place where the signal jumped the tracks

follow the wires, the guy had said
but maybe he'd lied   maybe the wires

would lead us nowhere   looping endlessly
back on themselves   like a run-out groove

we got down on our knees in the shattered quartz
trying to listen through the fuzz

the frantic shirr of tiny wings
electrical shocks   as the bodies hit

burned up on our skin   *no trespassing*
glass dust   in our ears and eyes

red threads   in the palms of our hands
we scrambled back   down to the bridge

& the mocking laugh of the waterfall

Downstairs in the church was a whole collection of heavy-looking metal boxes with switches and dials, headsets and wires, each displaying its own mysterious name – the Amplifier Model C-30 (Manufactured and Distributed by A. Cross & Co. Ltd, Toronto / Montreal), the Bell & Howell Lumina 1.2, the Crestline Super-8. My favourite was the *Model SX-62*, manufactured by the Hallicrafters Company. Behind a thin sheet of glass it had a printed display marked out in a grid, with lines and numbers. Below the lines were phrases such as AMATEUR 10 METER or POLICE COASTAL GOV, and in one place POLICE POLICE POLICE POLICE, like someone trying to get through on a telephone. In the spaces between the lines there were long lists of names – London, Paris, San Francisco; Vatican, Bucharest, Schenectady. I spent hours learning these names, the patterns they made read down or across. You could put them together in different ways, work out which combinations sounded best – Cincinnati, Honolulu, Venezuela, Edmonton. Some of the names I wasn't sure how to pronounce, but since there was no one to correct me, it didn't matter. Sometimes I turned the dials and flicked the switches, from RECEIVE to STANDBY, NOISE LIMITER OFF. They made a satisfying click, but of course nothing else ever happened. I tried to imagine all those places talking to one another, all those voices weaving in and out and around each other, what Haiti might say to Stockholm, or Canton to Alaska. It seemed an extraordinary sort of magic that all those places could be contained and connected within this grey metal box.

STORM

saturday 7 september / so here we are in the new world / and a storm is yammering at all four sides of our small square house / rattling the sashes / setting the rockingchair emptily rocking meaninglessly rocking / the power is out / the lines brought down / somewhere between here and the coast / by the wind that is like a gleeful child / with handfuls of new broken toys / a child that yells for the joy of yelling / and is much too strong for anyone to quieten

we cannot use any of our familiar machines / there is nothing for us to do but wait / there is a strange quiet under the storm / the quiet of time we need not fill / the quiet of time we can do nothing with / we spread out our hands / to show each other they are empty / a gesture of acceptance / of having come for a while to the end of things

AFTERMATH

Hit by the come-down, not knowing
what else to do, I walked down
to the river. It too

was changed, the flat rock
where I'd sat in the heat
of two days ago

now wholly submerged
and the river running fast and deep
and dark brown, much too deep

to see down to the stones. My mind
was still full of the rush
of the storm, its charged-up life

as it beat around us, the small house
like a hollow drum and the two of us
held inside it, the taste on the tongue

of the rough music, its rasp
in our throats, till our devices ran down
and there was nothing to do but

try to sleep. All through the night
the boards of the house groaned overhead
like the decks of a ship

and in the morning I fetched up alone,
the house still and cold and saying nothing,
last night's world not speaking to me

and the storm long passed, though the river now
says over and over *it was real, it did happen – listen*
to the deep new song of me, take it with you

and make it your own

BATTERY, CHAPEL POINT, SYDNEY MINES

broken walls   concrete foundations
spray-tag insignia   dazzle-paint

ROANE 6   MARCO   DANTE
MAX   MADDY   FORREST   REMEMBER

broken ground thick with grasses   wild currants
& blueberries   good foraging here
at the back of summer

broken steps   bunkers   tunnels
a place of levels

& at its heart the gun emplacement

curved chamber   passage tomb
stone leaking its own secrets   slow white
calcium drip

above in the sunlight   brilliant with rust
& verdigris   magic circle   gun mounting

clock face set with jewels
twelve teardrops of shattered glass
mosaic   mandala   almanac

electrical chatter in the long grass
sensed presence of sunsharp eyes
keeping watch over the bay

the toy lighthouse out on the Point
& the white ship heading north
to the open sea   & Newfoundland

GLACE BAY

End of the continent – nothing left
ahead but sea. Past the mining museum,

down on the shore, I found something
I couldn't name – made of metal,

about the fit and weight in the hand
of a pocket-knife, burnished and pocked

as though hallmarked, split open
along one side like a razor-shell

and jammed with jewels – tiny blocks
of yellowish stone, like citrine quartz

or rock sugar. No way to know
what it might have been, but now a gift,

 a souvenir – perfect, and puzzling,
and mine to keep.

UNCHARTED

UNCHARTED

Mornings don't exist any more.
In the afternoons, she climbs through the ruins
of the old Spanish fort. She's a young man

who's been sold a line about a city of gold,
about the way one thing leads smoothly
to another. But this is a place

of false trails, dead ends.
Again and again she runs through the rooms,
again and again she climbs the walls,

a young man clinging by his fingers
to the crumbling stone parapets.
Each time she falls, the world greys out,

clicks, reboots. She gets angry with the hints.
What fucking use is that,
she yells at the screen, *I already know*

where I'm trying to go, but I don't know how.
Back again to the room with the map,
back past the room with the broken floor.

All of this is just distraction,
surface-level misdirection
while something deeper reconfigures.

POOL / EMPTY

Indecent – the wrong side of a thought.
The awful white depth of it. Whitish trails
down the walls. Fur on the tongue.

A space never meant to be seen, never meant
to be emptied out. Steep white angled cliff,
halfway along – could you climb it?

Shiny aluminium steps, clamped to the wall
at the deep end. Three, four silver rungs,
smooth, logical, leading you on

by implication – here, yes, now here,
one step leads to the next, your foot
feeling the air, then blammo, nothing –

SHORE

Sick of the racket, the machinations,
sick of the parties and the family romance,

he came down to the shore and here he stands,
under a sky vaster than any

he's ever seen, a twisting play
of pale cloud, black gaps

like ragged holes torn in a backcloth.
Over the sea, the moon rising

inside its own gleaming arch,
spilling light the colour of rust

onto the sand, and facing him
his own white shadow, pale double,

speaking nothing, but mirroring
in dumb show his every move

– he blinks, hard, and the figure is gone.
Somewhere behind him, muffled cries,

the world still going its ways
hell for leather through the night.

But here there is only the low hiss
of the tide at his feet, the torn sky,

and the cold burning eye of the moon,
that says to him, *Well, and now that you know,*

what do you plan to do about it?

SOME DAY BEHIND US

seven of us with our books and maps
around the table

she said you know in some places
they say the future's back there

they say *tomorrow* is *some day behind us*

like the quietest child creeping towards us
as we stand blindfold, swivelling round
like a compass needle

until all at once the smash and grab
the lightning raid of kids like birds

because that's the game
because now, it's time

Out beyond the edge of the trees, sudden chaos of shape and colour, grey/brown/white – three dogs, running on the sand path. Then singular, upright, loping along, self-contained in his black clothes, drawn tight inside himself – the man of the dogs.

I know you, I said, & knew it only as I said it, some memory trying to rise – low ceilings, painted walls, talk, food smells, condensation, the rich dense mix of it, & this man at the centre of things, capable.

I hadn't meant to say it, I felt the bluntness, the intrusion of it, as though I'd staked a claim, thrown a kind of loop around him. I wanted to take it back, let him pass unremembered, unidentified, but it had seemed so important, that recognition, that connection back to another life, I had spoken it before I'd understood. & now we were caught, stopped on the sand path, while the dogs patterned and interwove, wanting away.

Yes, he said, *we come here often, they can run for miles on these dry tracks. We can walk for hours and see no-one.*

I pictured him down on the beach: single dark vertical line, three dark dots at his heels, trace on a screen.

remember the birds, in the chapel walls
the unexpectedness of them
the sudden lovely aliveness of them
in the place of the dead

swifts, I said
more likely martins
but I wanted swifts, because of the name

outside, the heat
and the young girl by the pond
who took off her shirt to run with her brothers
through the thin cool fall of the fountain

DRIFT LAYER

early in the sequence
far down in the drift layer

what did we do then
who   really   were we

we have lost that language now

the objects –

we examine them   we do our best
but in the end we shake our heads
we can't remember

*

in the drift layer   things move around
are not where we thought them

sandblow   alluvium   the landscape alters

going over and over disturbed ground
the record is unreliable

*

on the floodplain you find her
digging in the wet earth
looking for what the water brought

she opens her hand   palmful of shining stones
you reach out   she scatters them
in a wide arc back to the water

*

we are late now

so late in the sequence
we can't realise how late we are

when we sleep   we are barely below the surface
a thin layer covers us
the wind will soon sweep it away

*

small black cubes of sea-coal

blank dice picked from the sand
brought home in a pocket
tumbled together

wasn't it a game once

small cubes of china clay
knucklebones   jacks   dibs

two children scrambling
as they try to learn the trick of it

the quick fluid flick of the wrist

over and over

EIGHTEEN

the river is a mirror   a still thing
hiding its lethal machinery
of sandbanks and channels

the city invisible from where we stand
as though not yet come into being
or already existed and passed away

as though nothing now but these shining miles
all the way to the sea

you pose for a picture
arms outflung   as though to say
all this –   so much –

smile awry   as though to say
what is it you are leaving me –

late September

                       afternoon tilting down
        into the west

took off our boots
        walked through the shallows

unexpected warmth of the water
        like touching something you shouldn't touch

                         & not waves but thinnest layers
        sliding in & sliding in

white feet like flatfish
                soft mud plushing up
        settling back

skirting cordgrass
        stiff thin green blades
                      (imagine the slice –
     imagine the blood's warm bloom –)

black-headed gulls massing for take-off
                 fast low overhead

           tight turn into the sun
      & back down to land

& all the while the pulse of it
        the trough & push

      as afternoon dips its wing
to the red horizon

Nightfall is beautiful here.

Every evening, I leave the hut and walk up one of the tracks, around the edge of the opencast, heading for the stump of the old windmill on the ridge. Sometimes I take the seaward path, sometimes the landward. It doesn't matter – they meet at the old mill anyway. As the sun goes down, over the sea, the low light makes the stone glow, the heaps of it, the broken pieces of the heart of the mountain. They glow like precious stones, orange and yellow, turquoise and green, the oxide colours seeming to draw down the last slants of sunlight and come into new life, stone flowers that bloom at sunset. As though this spoil-heap were a new kind of garden.

On the ridge, leaning against the warm stone of the old mill, I look out towards the other island, the low grey mound of it, Holy Island, they called it, a bleak place of schist and scree and thin turf. I went there, once, to see the birds on the far side, the seaward side. Lay on my belly on the edge of the cliff and watched for a long while, the whole cliff covered with the white of them, and the air full of their scream and squabble, a constant crazy coming and going, a madhouse of birds. I was happy to come away in the end, back to the quiet of this used-up place, *my* mountain.

As the sun drops into the sea and the light fails, I stand looking across towards the island, trying to make out the long line of the harbour wall. Where the green lights of the marker buoys used to blink, and behind them the brighter lights of the docks, the town at night a shining thing across the water. Four times a day the big white ships would head out, you could set your watch by them. The waves they made across the bay would fetch all the kids down to the beaches, they knew the times and they'd be ready, riding the long roll of the waves that came for just those few minutes. Then the water would settle back again and the kids would disappear.

I don't know how long I stand there for, but I notice it's dark now, the bats are out, flitting and diving above my head. In and out of the broken mill, down to the opencast, to the edge of the water, making circuits like tiny airborne racing-drivers, then darting back in through the gaps in the walls. Sometimes I think I can hear them, too, chittering away in their high voices, like children, the way the children would call to each other when we climbed the hill in the evenings, how they'd always be discovering things in the long grass – a caterpillar, a beetle, maybe the bones of some creature – and they'd call to us, come and see, come and see, and the whole mountain was alive and singing with discovery

and I turn and the broken pieces of stone slide under my heel, the colours quite gone in the dark now, and I start to walk back down the path, back to the hut and the single light I've left burning.

RETURN

we take down the storm shutters   pale sea-light floods the rooms
wooden floorboards   the rooms quite bare   we walk through them
try the switches   generator somewhere back in the dunes
we make coffee   we walk through the rooms   boards creak
under our feet   hollow drum sound of the crawlspace
hiss & scritch against the porch   whisper of sand
its constant fetch against the shingles   spring and creak
of the kitchen floor   as we unpack the food
stock up the cupboards   rattle of glasses on the dresser
sudden burst of radio voices   kids' voices   some station
along the coast   maybe hundreds of miles   maybe not far
signal fading in & out   wind rising   green flare of the lamps
as we light them   snatch of radio harmony   *Surf City /*
here we come   & under it all the sea-murmur
unbroken thought of this place   out beyond the mudflats
sea observes   weighs things up   begins to think of coming home

NOTES

'Under the Lightship'
Based on a photograph of Dundee harbour by Gordon Morris
(viewed upside-down); thanks to Bill Herbert, who retweeted
the photograph.

'Long Grass with Butterflies'
Vincent van Gogh, *Long Grass with Butterflies* (oil on canvas,
1890).

'Seasons of the Hospital'
Vincent van Gogh, *Hospital at Saint-Rémy* (oil on canvas,
1889); *Pollarded Willows, Arles* (oil on canvas, 1888); *Trunk of
an Old Yew Tree* (oil on canvas, 1888); *A Corner of the Garden
at St Paul's Hospital, Saint-Rémy* (graphite and ink on paper,
1889).

'Corridor'
Vincent van Gogh, *Corridor in the Asylum* (chalk and diluted
oil on paper, 1889).

'Cypress'
Vincent van Gogh, *The Starry Night* (oil on canvas, 1889).

'Concession à perpetuité'
French text taken from https://www.service-public.fr/
particuliers/vosdroits/F31001

'Natural History'
The video referred to is in the 'Beginnings' gallery of the
National Museum of Scotland, Edinburgh.

'Nova Scotia'
Reworked versions of some of the poems in this section will form part of a collaborative text/sound work with Martin Heslop, forthcoming from Longbarrow Press. The poems are printed here in their original forms, as they were written during a two-week residency at the Elizabeth Bishop House, Great Village, Nova Scotia, in September 2019.

'Uncharted'
Based on the computer game *Uncharted: Drake's Fortune* (Naughty Dog/Sony Computer Entertainment, 2007).

'Shore'
Frederick James Shields, *Hamlet and the Ghost* (oil on canvas, 1901).

'Nightfall, Parys Mountain'
Parys Mountain, near Amlwch, Anglesey, is the site of a former copper mine. This piece is also partly inspired by the Duran Duran track 'Planet Earth' (1981).

ACKNOWLEDGEMENTS

Thanks to the editors of the following publications, where some of these poems were originally published: *The Abandoned Playground*; *Anthropocene*; *Bad Lilies*; *Bath Magg*; *Finished Creatures*; *M58*; *Magma*; *Poetry Review*; *Poetry Wales*; *Shearsman*.

'Amber' was commended in the Newcastle Poetry Competition 2019.

A version of 'Seasons of the Hospital' was longlisted in the Artlyst Art to Poetry Competition 2020.

'Sudley Field' was commissioned by Almanac Arts for the Liverpool RISE Festival in 2019, and was originally produced as a limited edition of 30 handmade booklets, designed in collaboration with Sarah Hymas (https://almanacarts.com/).

'Nightfall, Parys Mountain' was published as part of Manchester Metropolitan University's 'Write Where We Are Now' project in 2020 (https://www.mmu.ac.uk/write/).

The Nova Scotia poems were written during a two-week residency (with sound artist Martin Heslop) at the Elizabeth Bishop House, Great Village, Nova Scotia, in September 2019; I am grateful to the Elizabeth Bishop Society of Nova Scotia, especially Laurie Gunn, and to Liverpool John Moores University for financial support.

I am grateful to everyone at Carcanet Press, and to everyone who has generously discussed aspects of this book with me: Tara Bergin, Lucy Burnett, Cathy Cole, Rebecca Goss,

Caroline Hawkridge, Martin Heslop, Seán Hewitt, Holly Howitt-Dring, Andrew Kirk, Grevel Lindop, Carola Luther, Sarah Maclennan, John McAuliffe, Andrew McMillan, Callan Waldron-Hall, and most particularly Sarah Hymas and Judith Willson. And special thanks to Richard Monks for suggesting that I stay at the Quaker Hotel.